The Bear Went Over the Mountain

The
Child's
World®

Distributed by The Child's World®
1980 Lookout Drive • Mankato, MN 56003-1705
800-599-READ • www.childsworld.com

Acknowledgments
The Child's World®: Mary Berendes, Publishing Director
The Design Lab: Kathleen Petelinsek, Design

Library of Congress Cataloging-in-Publication Data
Dorenkamp, Michelle.
 The bear went over the mountain / illustrated by Michelle Dorenkamp.
    p. cm.
 ISBN 978-1-60954-295-5 (library bound : alk. paper)
 1. Children's songs–Texts. [1. Bears—Songs and music. 2. Songs.] I. Title.
 PZ8.3.D7337Be 2011
 782.42—dc22
 [E]   2010032421

Printed in the United States of America in Mankato, Minnesota.
December 2010
PA02074

ILLUSTRATED BY MICHELLE DORENKAMP

The bear went over the mountain,

the bear went over the mountain,

the bear went over the mountain,

to see what he could see.

And all that he could see,

and all that he could see was . . .

the other side of the mountain,

the other side of the mountain,

the other side of the mountain,

was all that he could see.

SONG ACTIVITY

**The bear went over the mountain,
the bear went over the mountain,
the bear went over the mountain,
to see what he could see.**

(Pretend you are climbing up a mountain.)

**And all that he could see,
and all that he could see was . . .**

(Put your hand above your eyes like you
are looking around.)

**the other side of the mountain,
the other side of the mountain,
the other side of the mountain,
was all that he could see.**

(Pretend you are now climbing down the
mountain. At the end of the song, shrug
your shoulders.)

BENEFITS OF NURSERY RHYMES AND ACTIVITY SONGS

Activity songs and nursery rhymes are more than just a fun way to pass the time. They are a rich source of intellectual, emotional, and physical development for a young child. Here are some of their benefits:

❋ Learning the words and activities builds the child's self-confidence—"I can do it all by myself!"

❋ The repetitious movements build coordination and motor skills.

❋ The close physical interaction between adult and child reinforces both physical and emotional bonding.

❋ In a context of "fun," the child learns the art of listening in order to learn.

❋ Learning the words expands the child's vocabulary. He or she learns the names of objects and actions that are both familiar and new.

❋ Repeating the words helps develop the child's memory.

❋ Learning the words is an important step toward learning to read.

❋ Reciting the words gives the child a grasp of English grammar and how it works. This enhances the development of language skills.

❋ The rhythms and rhyming patterns sharpen listening skills and teach the child how poetry works. Eventually the child learns to put together his or her own simple rhyming words— "I made a poem!"

ABOUT THE ILLUSTRATOR

Michelle Dorenkamp has been an illustrator for 25 years. She has created over 50 books, and loves every minute of her job! She lives near St. Louis, Missouri, and enjoys spending free time outdoors—especially with her granddaughter, Katlyn.